A word from the coach

Listen up, team. I'm proud of all of you, you've achieved beautiful writing so far. Now it's time to step up to the plate and start running.

You've been well-prepared in the junior league, so it will be easy to start joining. Use your entries and exits to help you flow. No bouncing, no jerking, just beautiful fluent movement and writing.

I'm sure you all know about cursive – it means *running* in ancient Latin. Those old Romans knew a thing or two about writing, and then in the 1700s a *cursor* was someone who ran messages. So you are joining a long tradition of running and writing.

Let's get out there and practise!

First drill: join the letters in your name. Take your time, think about it, and then go for it!

Second drill: review your first performance, decide how to improve, and go again!

Contents and curriculum links

Page number		Content	Eng Language	Eng Literature	Eng Literacy	History	Maths	Science	Other
1		*A word from the coach*		•	•	•			H & P E
2		Contents and curriculum links			•				
3		Pen and posture	•		•				
4		Concepts of writing	•		•				
5		Victorian Modern Cursive – Aspects of style	•		•				
6		Instructions: Letter formation	•		•				
7		Instructions: Downward letter formation	•		•				
8		Reference: Starting point and direction	•		•				
9		Revision: Unjoined writing	•		•				Geog
10		Techniques for joining – Diagonal joins	•		•				
11		Techniques for joining – Horizontal joins	•		•				
12		Techniques for joining – No joins; touch joins	•		•				
13		Techniques for joining – Joining to ascenders	•		•				
14		Practising touch joins	•		•				
15	a	Anagrams	•		•			•	
16	b	Early flight	•		•	•		•	Tech
17	c	Meanings of community	•		•	•			Geog
18	d	Diplodocus	•		•	•		•	
19	e	Spelling rule	•		•				
20	f	Flora and fauna	•		•			•	
21	g	Shopping in the past	•		•	•			
22	h	*Honey* poem	•	•	•			•	
23	i	Different indexes	•		•				Tech/ICT
24	j	Patrick Johnson	•		•	•	•		H & P E
25	k	Prefix kilo-	•		•		•	•	
26	l	States of matter	•		•			•	
27	m	Prefix mono-	•		•		•		
28	n	Suffix -ness	•		•				
29	o	Onomatopoeia	•		•				
30	p	Penguin jokes	•		•				
31	q	Nonsense poem	•	•	•				
32	r	Red herring	•	•	•				
33	s	Sprouting seeds	•		•			•	
34	t	Torus	•		•		•		
35	u	Ukulele	•		•				Arts
36	v	Velcro	•		•	•		•	
37	w	*Where?* Poem	•	•	•				
38	x	Prefix ex-	•		•				
39	y	Sydney to Hobart yacht race	•		•	•	•	•	Tech
40	z	Zoologist and zookeeper	•		•			•	
41	WYO	Sporting words	•		•				H & P E
42	Nos.	Equations	•		•		•		
43	WYO	Jokes	•		•				
44	WYO	Crossword	•		•				
45	WYO	ATH story	•		•				
46	Nos.	Times of the day	•		•		•		
47	WYO	A *Start Here* story	•		•				
48		End of year assessment	•		•				

WYO = Write Your Own page

Pencil hold

Hold your pencil like this. Hold it lightly so your hand doesn't get tired. Your index finger should be about 2 cm from the tip of the pencil.

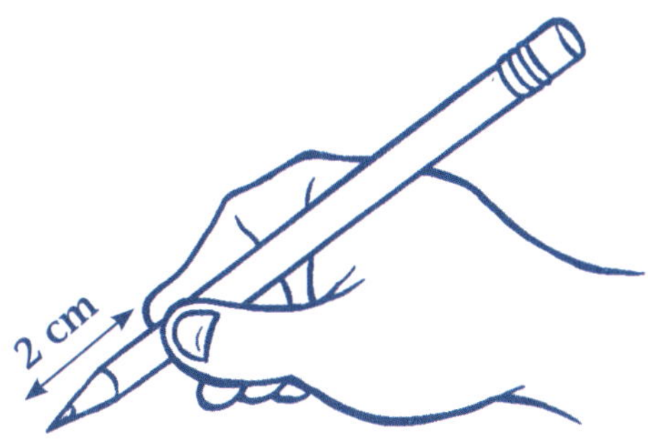

Pencil or pen

You could try using ballpoint and nylon-tipped pens as well as pencils this year. Try to find a tool that helps you to write well.

Posture

Sit comfortably.

Sit facing your desk, or turn slightly. Turn your paper also. Lean your body forward slightly from the hips but try not to touch the front of your desk. Rest both forearms on the desk.

Right-handers sit like this.

Keep your hand below the writing line so that you can see what you are writing. Rest your other arm on the desk.

Try not to write across your body. Keep the paper on the side of your body that you write with.

Left-handers

If you are left-handed you may prefer to write straight up and down, but you should try not to write backhand.

If you sit the correct way and slant your paper, you should be able to see your work clearly.

Left-handers sit like this.

Concepts of writing

Writing is made up of letters and words.

English has 26 letters. They can be written in CAPITALS or lower case.

a h m y

B F P Z

Letters make different sounds in different words.

Spaces between the words make it easier to read the writing.

coat shoes jumper hat

wearing warm clothes

Sentences

A sentence is a group of words that makes a whole thought or idea.

Sentences start with a capital letter and usually end with a full stop or a question mark. Some sentences end with an exclamation mark for emphasis.

It's raining!

How long will it last?

We have to go inside.

The dam will fill up.

Victorian Modern Cursive – Aspects of style

1 Most letters start at the **top** and have strong **downstrokes**.

2 Most letters have **crisp turns**. This makes a **wedge** shape in many letters.

3 Many letters have **exits** and some have **entries**. This makes it easier to do joined writing.

4 The writing has a slight **slope** to help with fluency. (You may write straight up and down if you prefer.)

5 All letters have a **body**. Some also have a **head** (or ascender) and a **tail** (or descender). The letter **f** has all three.

6 All of these aspects help with **joined writing**. Entries and exits become the joins between the letters. Strong downstrokes and crisp turns help the writing to move forward. Pen lifts and touch joins help in writing long words.

See pages 6 to 8 for more about letter formation.
See pages 10 to 13 for more about joins.

Instructions: Letter formation

Anti-clockwise letters a c g q d e o f s

a c g q	Start at the top (1 o'clock). Move anti-clockwise. Finish letters **a** and **q** with an exit.
d e	Start in the middle. Move anti-clockwise. Finish with an exit.
o f s	Start at the top. Move anti-clockwise. Letter **o** has an exit. Letter **f** has a tail and two strokes.

Clockwise letters m n r x z h k p

m n r	Start with a small entry. Move down, then clockwise. Finish with an exit.
x z	Start with a small entry. Move clockwise. Letter **x** has two strokes. Letter **z** has a flattened tail.
h k p	Start at the top. Move down, then clockwise. Finish with an exit.

Downward letters: the *i* family   i l t j

i l t

Start at the top.
Move ↓ downwards.
Finish with an exit.
Letter **t** has two strokes.

j

Start at the top.
Move ↓ downwards.
Finish with a flattened tail.

Downward letters: the *u* family   u v w b y

u v w b

Start at the top.
Move ↓ downwards.
Use crisp turns.
Finish with an exit.

y

Start at the top.
Move ↓ downwards.
Finish with a flattened tail.

Reference: Starting point and direction

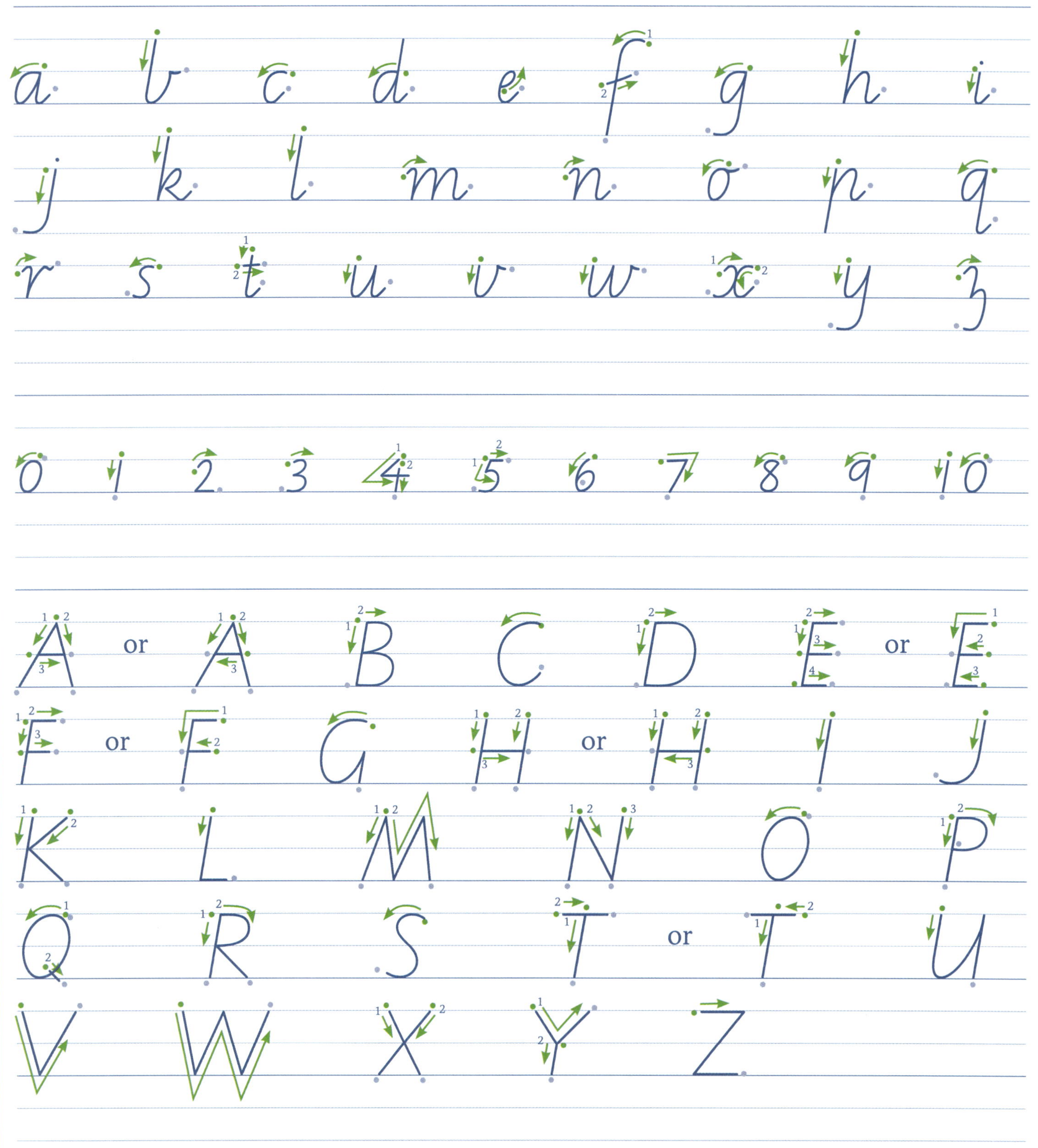

• starting point ↓ direction • finishing point

CAPITALS: alternative formations are for left-handers.

Revision: Unjoined writing

Date ____________

Self-assess

Albany

Bourke

Cooktown

Derby

Eildon

Foster

Goolwa

Hawker

Innamincka

Jerilderie

Katherine

Launceston

Mt Isa

EXTRA: What resources could you use to find place names starting with N – Z?

Date ____________

Diagonal joins **After a c d e h i k l m n p q s t u x**

Join at the top of the next letter's body.
Stay at the same angle as the exit.
This makes a wedge shape between the letters.

in → in

am	am	came
ce	ce	cell
do	do	done
en	en	ten
hi	hi	hit
is	is	this
kn	kn	know
lo	lo	hello
me	me	meal
nn	nn	Jenny
pl	pl	play

Date ____________

qu qu quads

sh sh shell

tr tr train

ul ul pull

xe xe pixel

Horizontal joins **After b f o r v w**

Join at the top of the next letter's body. ou → ou

br br brown

fl fl flies

or or more

ru ru run

ve ve seven

wo wo won

Date ___________

No joins **After g j y z**

(You might use speed loops after these letters later on.)

go go goat

je je jet

ya ya yam

zo zo zone

Touch joins (or pen lifts)

Lift your pen and drop the next letter in.
Always use touch joins before **a c d g q**.

ea → ea

Also use touch joins when you write long words.

ta ta taste

oc oc sock

ed ed tried

ug ug mug

aq aq aqua

Date ____________

Self-assess

Joining to ascenders   Before b h k l t

1 Stay at the angle of the exit to the top of the body.
2 Change to the angle of the downstroke.
3 Go up to the top of the ascender.
4 Come down with a strong downstroke.

rl → rl

From diagonal exits

ab ab about

ch ch peach

nk nk sink

el el smell

ut ut nut

From horizontal exits

ob ob job

wh wh why

rk rk park

bl bl cable

ft ft raft

Remember: the join to letter **d** (the only other letter with an ascender) is a touch join.

Date ____________

Self-assess

ear hear

par party

tch watch

end send

ied tried

ing doing

equ equal

Write your name. Circle any places where you need to use touch joins.
Then write your name again.

Write your teacher's name. Check for touch joins,
and then write the name again.

EXTRA: Find interesting long words to write out, using touch joins where necessary.

Date ____________

Self-assess

a a A A

Diagonal joins from a

Always touch join to a

ai as at ba la sa

Spelling: Add-a-letter

ant → aunt can → can't

Fluency: Word fun

Anagrams

astronomer = moon starer

a telescope = to see place

traffic rules = careful first

EXTRA: Spell out this equation to make an anagram: 12 + 1 = 11 + 2

Date ______________

Self-assess

b b

B B

Horizontal joins from b

bi bo by

Joins to b

eb mb ob

Spelling: Add-a-letter

be → bet → best / beat → beast

Fluency: Early flight

Hot air balloons

- the earliest way to fly
- 1783: first manned flight,

in Paris, France

EXTRA: Research the invention of hot-air balloons.

Date ______________

c c

C C

Diagonal joins from c

ca ch cr

Always touch join to c

ec ic oc

Self-assess

Spelling: Special foods

cake chocolate ice-cream

Fluency: Meanings of community

A community – people who live in a local area, or have things in common, or share values or ideas.

EXTRA: What communities do you belong to?

Date ____________

d d D D

Diagonal joins from d

de do dy

Always touch join to d

ed id od

Spelling: Anagrams

dare → read drive → diver

Fluency: Dinosaurs

Diplodocus

- plant-eating dinosaur
- first fossils collected in

North America in 1877

EXTRA: What does the diagram show? What is unrealistic about it?

Date ______________

Self-assess

e e

E E

Diagonal joins from e

eg en ey

Joins to e

he re se

Spelling: Words in words

empties – pies step site

Fluency: Spelling rule

I before E except after C

pie piece

ceiling

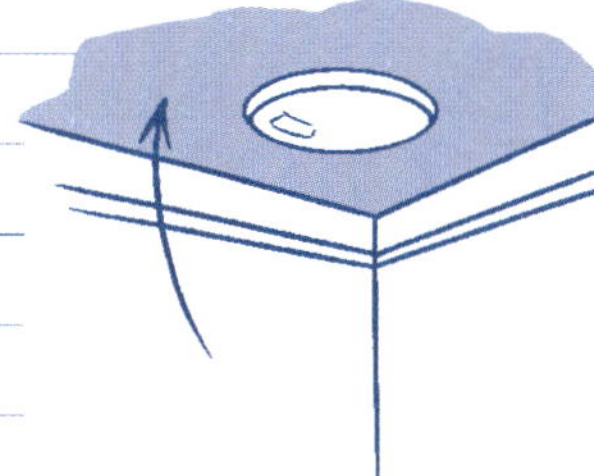

die diesel

receive

field sieve

receipt

EXTRA: Add more words to each list. Which list is longer? Why?

Date ____________

f f

F F

Horizontal joins from f

fe fl fu

Joins to f

af if of

Spelling: Words in words

toffee: fee feet of off toe

Fluency: Definitions

Flora (e.g. wattle)

Fauna (e.g. emu)

– the plants and animals

of a certain place or time.

EXTRA: Make a list – The Flora and Fauna at our school.

Date ______________

Self-assess

g g No join after g

G G Always touch join to g

ga gh gr eg ig ng

Spelling: Colours

green grey gold orange

Fluency: Shopping in the past

Before supermarkets

the grocer sold dry goods,

the greengrocer sold greens,

and the butcher sold meat.

EXTRA: Make a list of other things these three shopkeepers sold.

Date ______________

h h

H H

Diagonal joins from h

ha hi hu

Joins to h

ch sh th

Spelling: Change-a-letter

head → heat hole → home

Fluency: *Honey* poem

Honeycomb hexagons

Oozing runny honey.

Food for bee larvae –

Or us hungry humans.

EXTRA: What is honey? How do bees make it?

Date ____________

Self-assess

i i

l l

Diagonal joins from i

ib im is

Joins to i

di li oi

Spelling: Words in words

inside: in din side dine

Fluency: Different indexes

Index finger: points the way

Book or website index:

shows you where to find

information

EXTRA: What else can you use to find your way around a book or website?

Date ______________

j j No join after j

j j Joins to j

je jo ju aj ej oj

Spelling: Things I like

jam jeans jelly junk

Fluency: A famous Australian

Patrick Johnson – athlete

In 2003, he became the first

Australian to run 100 metres

in under 10 seconds.

EXTRA: Find out more about Johnson or another champion Australian athlete.

Date ___________

Self-assess

k k K K

Diagonal joins from k

ke ks ky

Joins to k

lk ok rk

Spelling: Silent k

know knit knot knew

Fluency: Word parts

Prefix kilo- thousand

1 kilogram = 1000 grams

1 kilometre = 1000 metres

1 kilolitre = 1000 litres

EXTRA: What is measured in kilograms? In kilometres? In kilolitres?

Date ____________

l l   L L

Diagonal joins from l

la ll ly

Joins to l

el ol pl

Spelling: Change-a-letter

lamp → limp → limb → lamb

Fluency: States of matter

Liquids need a container.

Solids keep their shape.

Ice (a solid) changes to

water (a liquid).

EXTRA: What causes solids to become liquids?

Date ____________

Self-assess

m m M M

Diagonal joins from m

me mi ms

Joins to m

lm om um

Spelling: Change-a-vowel

male → mile → mole → mule

Fluency: Prefix *mono-* means one or single

monorail – train

monohull – boating

monotone – music

monolith – landform

EXTRA: Find other words with the prefix *mono-*.

Date ____________

n n

N N

Diagonal joins from n

Joins to n

nd ni no an on rn

Spelling: Odd one out

name nest nine nothing

Fluency: Word parts

Suffix -ness means having the quality of. For example darkness, cleanliness, fitness, eagerness, laziness, sadness

EXTRA: What are the opposites of these *-ness* words?

Date ____________

Self-assess

o o

O O

Horizontal joins from o

oe on ot

Joins to o

do io ro

Spelling: Exclamations

Cooee! Oh! Boo! Ouch!

Fluency: Expressive words

Onomatopoeia – the sound

suggests the meaning

e.g. woof woof moo

meow tick tock

EXTRA: Make a list of onomatopoeic words. Make up some new ones as well!

Date ____________

p p

Diagonal joins from p

P P

Joins to p

pa pi ps ep rp up

Spelling: Animals

pig pony puppy elephant

Fluency: Jokes

1 How does a penguin

make pancakes?

2 Why do penguins carry

fish in their beaks?

1. With its flippers. 2. Because they don't have any pockets.

Date ___________

q q Diagonal joins from q

Q Q Always touch join to q

qu qu qu aq eq oq

Spelling: Odd one out

equal queen quite quit

Fluency: Nonsense poem

A quartet of quilters
sat quilting all week.
A quintet of squires
queued up for a peek.

EXTRA: Where can you see other quartets or quintets?

Date ____________

r r

R R

Horizontal joins from r

re ri ry

Joins to r

br fr ur

Spelling: Two-r words

rare roar Terry runner

Fluency: Meaning of an idiom

red herring

1 A fish that's been smoked

2 something to distract you,

a false clue

EXTRA: Have you read any mystery stories with red herrings in them?

Date ____________

Self-assess

s s

S S

Diagonal joins from s

se sl sp

Joins to s

as ls rs

Spelling: Compound words

sun set rise less shine

Fluency: Sprouting seeds

1 Soak bean seed overnight.

2 Slip off wrinkly coat.

3 Split seed in two.

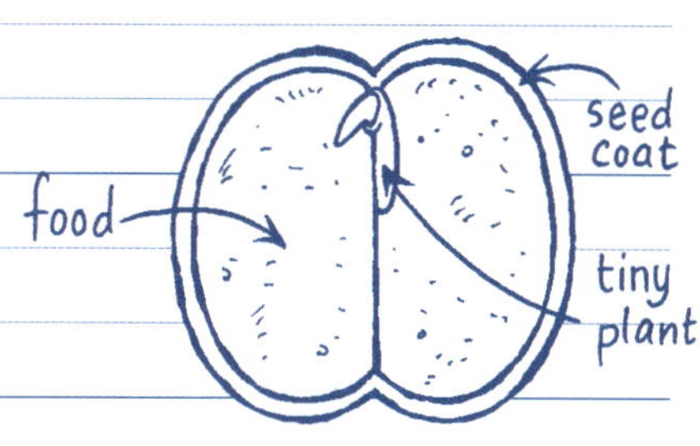

4 See the tiny plant inside.

EXTRA: Keep some whole soaked seeds moist for a few days. What happens?

Date ______________

t t T T

Diagonal joins from t

th to tt

Joins to t

et ft ut

Spelling: Days of the week

Tuesday Thursday Saturday

Fluency: A special object

Torus – 3D mathematical

object based on a circle

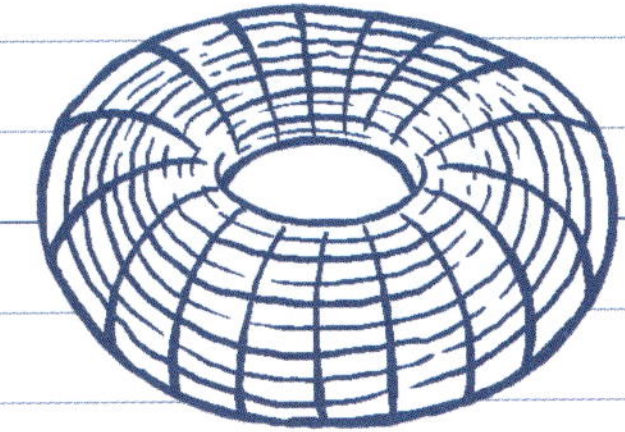

e.g. donut

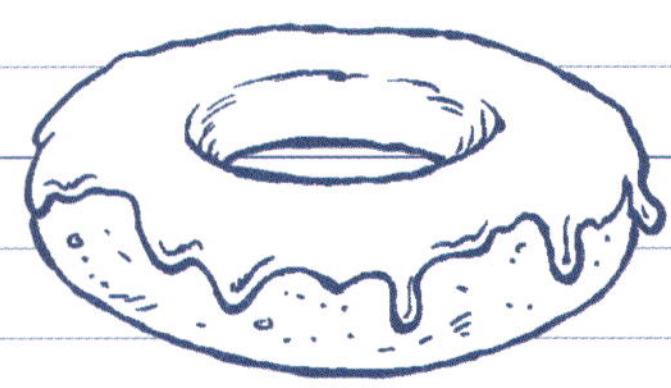

tyre inner-tube

EXTRA: What is your favourite torus-shaped object?

Date ____________

Self-assess

u u

U U

Diagonal joins from u

ud un ur

Joins to u

fu ru su

Spelling: What are the opposites?

under up ugly out buy

Fluency: Musical instrument

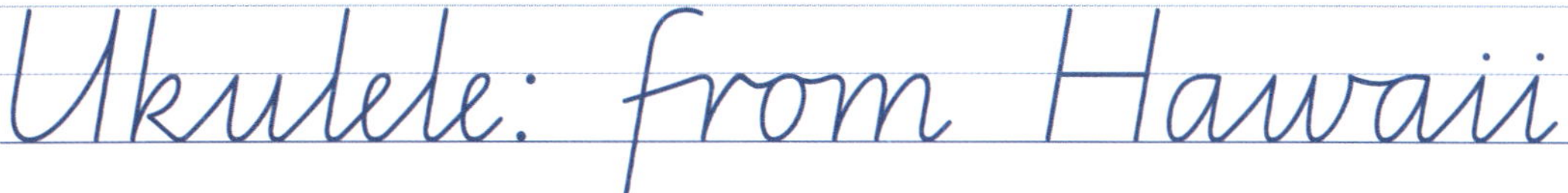

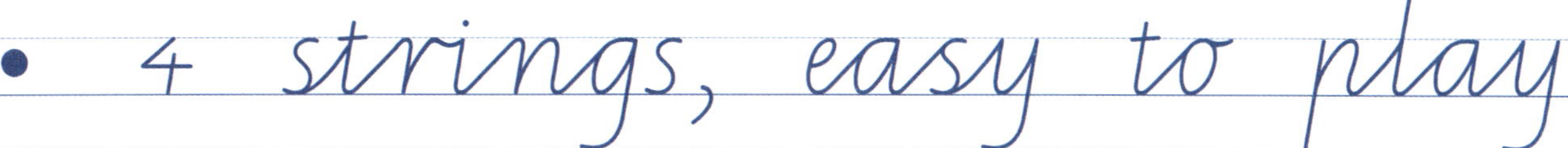

EXTRA: Listen to some music that uses one or more ukuleles.

Date ____________

v v

V V

Horizontal joins from v

va vi vo

Joins to v

av ev ov

Spelling: Odd one out

five river never very

Fluency: How Velcro works

Velcro: invented about 1950

One side has loops.

One side has hooks.

The hooks catch the loops.

EXTRA: Find out more about the invention of Velcro, and how it got its name.

Date ____________

w w W W

Horizontal joins from w

wh wi wr

Joins to w

aw ew ow

Spelling: Change-a-letter

was → wag wind → wand

Fluency: *Where?* poem

Is there a line where
the land joins the sea?
It's there on a map, but
at the beach, where is it?

Self-assess

EXTRA: Is it easy or hard to answer these two questions?

Date ______________

x x X X

Diagonal joins from x

xa xe xi

Joins to x

ax ex ox

Spelling: Rhyming words

axe Max wax packs

Fluency: Word parts

Prefix ex– out of, from

export – send goods out

exhale – breathe out

extend – stretch, draw out

EXTRA: Use other prefixes (e.g. *in*-, *pre*-, *trans*-) to change these words.

Date ____________

Self-assess

y y No join after y

Y Y Joins to y

ya ye yo ly ry ty

Spelling: Add two letters

yell → yellow you → young

Fluency

Sydney to Hobart yacht race

• getting faster every year

• starts 26 Dec.

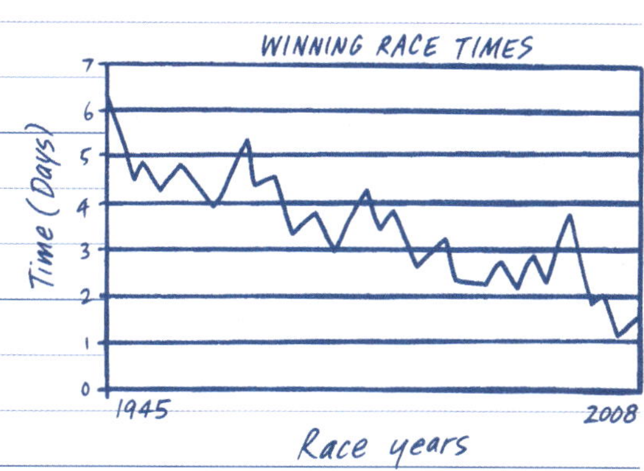

• takes ≥ 2 days

EXTRA: Why do you think that race times have been getting shorter?

Date ___________

z z No join after z

Z Z Joins to z

za ze zo az iz oz

Spelling: At the beach

zinc lazy hazy doze

Fluency: Occupations

Zoologist – studies living

beings

Zookeeper – looks after

animals in a zoo

EXTRA: List zoo-related words and find out their meanings.

Write your own: Sporting words

Date ______________

1 Add more words to this list of words about sports.

team score play

run first ball

2 What is your favourite sport?

3 Write words related to your favourite sport (e.g. football: *behind*, *mark*).

4 Write one or two sentences about playing your sport.

Self-assess

EXTRA: Write a magazine article about yourself as a top sportsperson.

Date ______________

Self-assess

Fill in the table with equations and a diagram.

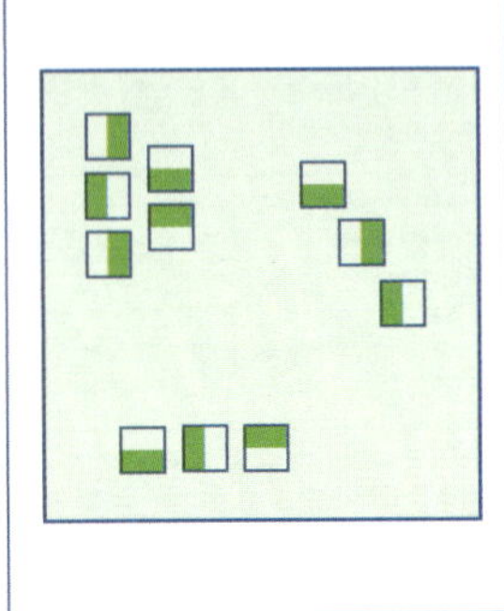	$3 + 2 + 2 + 3 + 2 + 2 = \square$ $2 + 2 + 2 + 2 + 3 + 3 = \square$ $(2 \times 3) + (4 \times \square) = \square$
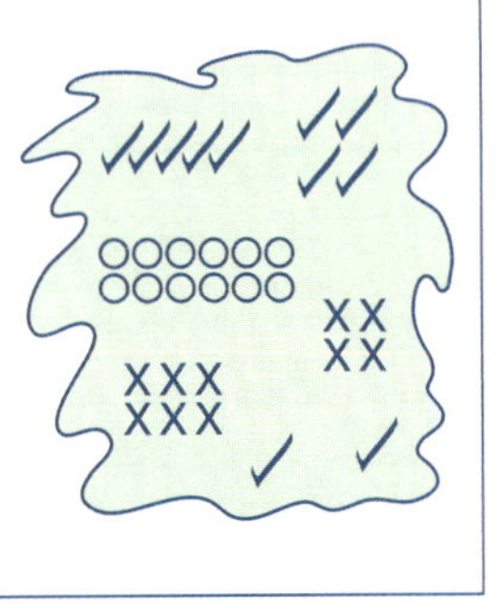	

	$6 + 2 + (3 \times 4) + 1 = \square$

EXTRA: Write equations about the items in your pencil case.

Date ___________

Self-assess

Lots of jokes and riddles depend on double meanings. Here are two:

1 *Did you see the man walking a lettuce? He thought it was a collie.*

2 *Bill: My favourite dinosaur is Tyrannosaurus Rex. Bet you can't spell that.*
Jill: Yes I can: T—H—A—T!

Rewrite one of these jokes in the box.

Write one of your own favourite jokes here.

EXTRA: Explain the double meanings in these jokes.

Date ______________

Self-assess

Across

1 Clocks and _____ show the time.
6 a ruler's special chair
7 _____ fi fo fum ...
8 place where chickens live
11 _____ and behold!
12 peaked hat
13 green pear-shaped fruit
15 $\frac{1}{2}$ of 20
16 white bone in the mouth
18 'house' made out of material
19 short for Susan
20 tall plant with a trunk

Down

2 left from burning wood
3 delicious brown sweets
4 *Write Well* author's name
5 97 – 96 =
6 $\frac{1}{4}$ of 48
7 special large meal
9 midday
10 2-wheeled fun vehicle
13 sounds like '8'
14 fried cake with hole
17 the piece missing from word 14

EXTRA: Write a new set of clues for this crossword.

Date ____________

weather
Kathryn
father
Nathan
leather
bath

ath

gather
Heath
path
bathroom
maths
feather

Write a story with many **ath** words.

You can add endings such as *-s*, *-ed*, *-ing* to these words.

Ask yourself these questions to help you plan your story.

Who? *When?*
Where? *What?*
Which? *Why?*
How?

EXTRA: Practise reading your story aloud and then read it to a friend.

Date ____________

What are you often doing at these times?

8:45 a.m.	
11:15 a.m.	
1:00 p.m.	eating my lunch
4:00 p.m.	
6:30 p.m.	

What is one time you usually do these things?

	School day	Weekend or holiday
brush teeth		
eat breakfast		10:00 a.m.
go to bed		
play with friends		
ride bike		
watch TV	7:00 p.m.	

EXTRA: Create a table that shows what you'd like to do on one special day.

Date ______________

Choose one thing from each box as a starting point for a story.

Setting	Characters	Events
☐ neighbour's house	☐ airline pilot	☐ burst water pipe
☐ shopping centre	☐ Aunty Jean	☐ birthday party
☐ space station	☐ five actors	☐ solar eclipse
☐ Greenland	☐ dentist	☐ school visit
☐ river bank	☐ Mr X	☐ excursion
☐ Uluru	☐ you	☐ robbery

EXTRA: Choose another set of *Start Here* items for another story to write or tell.

End of year assessment

1 Write your name in unjoined writing.

2 Write your teacher's name in capital letters.

3 Write this sentence in joined writing: The five boxing wizards jump quickly.

4 Write one or two sentences about the best thing you did on the weekend.